Azeri in the Republic of Azerbaijan is written in Latin script but Azeri in Iran is written in the Arabic script. Azeri in Iran is mostly spoken than written language but there is a number of literature that has been in this script.

Inside Iran, Azeri is commonly called as *Torki* with the language spoken in Turkey, this language is called *Estanbol Torki*, mean Istanbol Turkish.

This phrasebook uses English transliteration for writing Azeri words and phrases and thus, avoides teaching the script which would be difficult and time consuming. So, by using this phrasebook, you will be able to learn the practical and economical way of communicating in Azeri.

Abbreviations Used in This Chapter

n   noun

pol polite

sg   singular

pl   plural

PRONOUNCIATION

The pronunciation of Azeri is easy and straightforward. Unlike in English, there is a consistency between pronunciation and spelling. Stress is generally on the last syllable of the word as in *ä***qäj** 'tree'. However, the stress on proper nouns is on the first syllable as in *äy-din* 'Aydin'.

VOWELS

We can find nine vowels in Azeri. These vowels are presented in the following inventory:

	front		back	
	unround	round	unround	round
high	i	ü	ı	u
mid	e	ö		o
low	ä		a	

The vowel system in Azeri consists of nine vowels. These vowels are:

a   as the 'a' in 'ask' and 'fdi'

e   as the 'e' in 'get' and 'fell'

i   as the 'i' in 'fit' and 'pitch'

o   as the 'a' in 'ball' or the 'o' in 'mole'

u   as the 'u' in 'rule' and 'push'

ä   as the 'o' in 'top' or 'a' in 'father'

ü   as in "müde" is like a Scottish person saying "grew". (make the sound "ee" as in "cheese" and then make your lips into an "o" shape)

ö   as in "blöd" is like an English person saying "burn". (make the sound "a" as in the word "may" and then make your lips into an "o" shape)

ı   as the pronunciation of 'i' in New Zealand accent.

Vowel harmony in Azeri

All Turkic languages including Azeri have vowel harmony. In vowel harmony, all the vowels in a word assimilate to the preceding vowel with respect to certain phonetic features. For example the suffix for infinitive differ based on the preceding vowels, as in

gal-mak   'to come'

äl-mäx   to get'

Azeri (Azerbaijani) Phrasebook

Yavar Dehghani

INTRODUCTION

Azeri is a member of Turkic language group which itself is a subgroup of Altaic languages. Most Azeri speakers inhabit the four provinces in the north western parts of Iran, i.e. West Azerbaijan, East Azerbaijan, Ardabil and Zanjan, and the Republic of Azerbaijan. Iranian dialects of Azeri have been influenced heavily by Persian. A primary reason for this influence is that Persian and Azeri speakers have had the same nationality, religion and culture.

This phrasebook is based the Azeri dialects spoken in Iran and it is intended for the tourists who travel to these provinces where people speak Azeri, although the official language is Azeri. The equivalent Azeri words provided are the commonly used words and phrases, although most of them are borrowed from Persian. So, the intention here is not to provide the original Azeri word for each word but the one that is currently used by people on the streets. For example, the word *Haväpeymä is used for aeroplan* rather than *tayyära*, because people use the first word rather than the second one.

Learning Azeri has many benefits for foreign visitors. For example, by communicating in Azeri, they will be able to communicate effectively with the locals especially in remote areas where people are monolingual and do not know Persian very well. They can also find out about the culture and the history, and thus enjoy more visiting numerous monuments of the cities like Tabriz, Zanjan, Orumieh and Ardabil. By knowing Azeri, they will also be able to communicate with and understand the speakers of the related languages like Turkish. Although Azeri dialect of the Republic of Azerbaijan does not use many Persian words, and is influenced by Russian, you will still be able to communicate with them very well by using this phrasebook.

As we see, in the first one, the suffix is is *mak* because of harmony with *gal*, but in the second one, the suffix becomes *mäx* because of harmony with *äl*. So, for many suffixes and prefixes, there are two varities because of vowel harmony with the previous segment.

CONSONANTS

Most Azeri consonants are pronounced like their English counterparts. The consonants, which are pronounced similar to the English ones, are listed here:

b as the 'b' in 'boy'

ch as the 'ch' in 'cheese'

d as the 'd' in 'door'

f as the 'f' in 'feet'

j as the 'j' in 'jar'

m as the 'm' in 'me'

n as the 'n' in 'net'

s as the 's' in 'sin'

sh as the 'sh' in 'she'

t as the 't' in 'toy'

v as the 'v' in 'vest'

y as the 'y' in 'yes'

z as the 'z' in 'zip'

There are three consonants in Azeri, which do not exist in English. These consonants are:

x as the 'ch' in the Scottish 'loch'. It is pronounced at the back of the mouth, when the root of tongue makes a smooth contact with the end of the palate.

q, a guttural sound like a heavy French 'r', which is also pronounced at the back of the mouth, when the root of tongue makes a sudden contact with the end of the palate

zh as the 'zh' in 'Zhivago' or the 'g' in 'mirage'

' A glottal stop which is pronounced in the throat and marks a break in the flow of speech.

The following consonants are slightly different from their English counterparts:

l : Azeri l is pronounced in the front of the mouth, so it is similar to the 'l' in 'life', but not the 'l' in 'role'

k: It is similar to the English 'k' before and after 'a\-, u, o' but it is palatalised with 'i, e, a' which is similar to the 'ck' in 'backyard'

g: like 'k' has two forms: it is like the 'g' in 'got' before or after 'a\-, o, u', and similar to the 'g' in 'get' before or after 'a, e, i'

r: similar to a trilled 'r' in English but never silent or diphtongised.

h: as in the 'h' in 'hit'. It is never silent.

All Azeri consonants can be doubled where they are always pronounced distinctly as in 'hot tea' but not in 'kettle'

ACCENTS & DIALECTS

There are several dialects of Azeri such as Tarizi, Uromiyeyi, Ardabili, Zanjani, Bakuyi, etc. The main difference of these dialects is in phonological patterns like intonation, word stress and syllable reduction. The speakers of all these dialects can understand each other very well. However, they have vocabulary difference and some minor grammatical differences with the the Azeri spoken in Baku. The reason as mentioned above is that the dialects in Iran have been influenced heavily by Persian as the national language and education language throught the school and the language of media, and Persian words and phrases are more commonly used than Azeri ones by the speakers. On the other hand, in Baku, Azeri has always been an official spoken and written national language, although it has borrowed many words from Russian.

The difference between Azeri and other Turkic languages like Turkish, Turkman, Uzbak, etc. is more, and that is why, they are considered separate languages. However, Azeri and Turkish are closer to each other and the speakers of these two languages can communicate with each other effectively. So, by having this phrasebook, you can communicate with Turkish speakers as well.

GRAMMAR

Azeri is an inflectional and predominantly agglutinative language, that is, the verb is conjugated for person and number of the subject, and the words are attached to each other as suffixes. So, unlike in English, the subject can be omitted from the sentence, as in this example

I went home.   *man eva getdim*

        (lit: I-to home went-I)

The language system is much more easy and regular than English to learn and remember. This section will try to provide a simple and basic grammar of Azeri, although it can not cover all aspects of the grammar in these few pages.

WORD ORDER

The basic word order in Azeri is: subject, object, and verb, which is different from English. However, this order is not fixed especially in the spoken style where the verb can come before the object. Because the verb is conjugated for the subject, the subject can usually be omitted from the sentence. Thus, even if you can not remember the word order, Azeri speakers will understand you, no matter where in the sentence you tell the verb.

ARTICLES

Azeri has different means to express articles like 'the' and 'a/an'. The word *bir* 'one' before the noun conveys the meaning of the English article 'a/an'. For example:

I saw a boy in the street.   *bir oqlänı xiyäbändä gördüm*

        (lit: boy-a in the street saw-I)

I went to a hotel yesterday.   *dünan bir hotela getdim*

        (lit: yesterday to a hotel went-I)

Otherwise the noun is definite, as in:

I saw the musuem.   *man muzani gördüm*

        (lit: I museum saw-I)

NOUNS

Nouns in Azeri do not have gender. They are pluralised by adding *lär* to the end of the noun, as in:

book   *kitäb*

books   *kitäb-lär*

car   *mäshın*

cars   *mäshın-lär*

However, unlike in English, nouns in Azeri do not pluralise when they come after numbers more than one, as in:

'one house'   bir ev

'two houses'   iki ev

'ten houses'   on ev

Noun cases

Noun cases in Azeri are marked by a postposition. Each case shows the role of the noun in the sentence as a subject or object. There are six noun cases in Azeri.

Nominative case

The subject in the sentence always has a nominative case and it does not take any postposition, like *otubus* 'bus' in:

The bus left.   *otubus getdi*

        (lit: the bus went-it)

Accusative case

This case shows that the noun is the direct object of the sentence. It is formed by the postposition *(n)ι,* which comes after the noun, as in:

I saw Shiraz.   *man shiraz-ι gördüm*

                         (lit: I Shiraz saw-I)

I ate the apple.   *man älmä-nι yedim*

                         (lit: I apple ate-I)

Genitive case

The genitive case, conveys possession and ownership. To indicate a possession relation, the possessor takes a genitive case, while the possessed entity takes a possessive suffix, as in:

your ticket   *san-in bilit-in*

the city centre   *shahr-in markaz-i*

Dative case

This case is formed by adding the postposition *a* to the noun and indicates that the noun is an indirect object, as in:

I went to Tehran.   *man tehrän-ä getdim*

                         (lit: I to Tehran went-I)

Locative case

This case shows the location where an action takes place. It is formed by adding the postposition *dä* to the noun, as in:

Can I meet you in the hotel?   *San-i hotel-da gör-a-bilar-am?*

(lit: can-I you in the hotel see-I)

Ablative case

This case indicates the origin of an action. It is formed by adding the postposition *dan* to the noun, as in:

I came from Tabriz today.   *man bugün Tabriz-dan gal-dim*

(lit: I today from Tabriz came-I)

Pronouns

Because all Azeri verbs are conjugated for person and number of the subject, the subject pronouns, like nouns, can be omitted from the sentence. Unlike in English, the second person in Azeri has two forms: *san* for the singular and *siz* for the plural:

I	*man*	we	*biz*
you	*san*	you(pl)	*siz*
he/she/it *o*		they	*olär*

VERBS

Verbs in Azeri are conjugated for the person and number of the subject as well as for tense. Therefore, by adding the fixed set of suffixes to the verb root, you can easily make all forms of a verb. The verb root Azeri is formed by deleting the suffix *mak/mäx* from the infinitive. For example, the infinitive form for the verb 'to read' is *oxu-mäx* and its verb root *is oxu*. To form the past tense, we can simply add the past tense suffixes to this root:

I read.   *oxu-dum*

We read.   *oxu-dux*

Present tense

The present tense is formed by the suffix *ir* after the verb and adding the personal suffixes *am, san, ø, ik, siz, lar* to the end of the verb, as in these examples:

I read.   *ox-ur-äm*   We read.   *ox-ur-ux*

You read.   *ox-ur-sän*   You read (pl).   *ox-ur-suz*

He/she reads.   *ox-ur*   They read.   *ox-ur-lär*

Past Tense

Past tense is formed by adding the personal suffixes *dim, din, di, dik, diz, dilar* to the verb root, as in these examples:

I read.   *oxu-dum*   We read.   *oxu-dux*

You read.   *oxu-dun*   You(pl)read   *oxu-duz*

He/she/it reads.   *oxu-du*   They read.   *oxu-dulär*

Future Tense

To form the future, the verb root is conjugated with the personal suffixes, but the suffix *ajak/äjäx* comes between the root and the personal suffix. For example, *oxu-yäjäq-äm* 'I will read' is formed by adding *äjäx* between *oxu* and *äm*, as in these examples:

I will read.   *oxu-yäjäx-äm*

You will read.   *oxu-yäjäx-sän*

He/she will read. *oxu-yäjäx*

We will read.   *oxu-yäjäx-ıx*

You (pl) will read. *oxu-yäjäx-sız*

They will read.   *oxu-yäjäx-lär*

IMPERATIVE

The imperative form of a verb is formed by the verb root, as in: *ye* 'Eat!' and *oxu* 'Read!'.

The negative form of the imperative is formed by adding *mä* to the end of the verb root, as in:

Don't eat!   *ye-ma*

Don't read!   *oxu-mä*

TO BE

The *to be* verb in Azeri, like other verbs, is conjugated by adding the personal suffixes. This verb can be added to nouns, adjectives, or adverbs. For example, *susuz* plus *äm* means 'I am thirsty'.

I am thirsty.   *susuz-äm*

You are thirsty.   *susuz-sän*

He/she/it is thirsty.   *susuz-dı*

We are thirsty.   *susuz-ux*

You(pl) are thirsty.   *susuz-suz*

They are thirsty.   *susuz-dulär*

COMPOUND VERBS

In Azeri, there are a large number of compound verbs which are formed by a noun or an adjective followed by a simple verb form like *elamak* 'to do', and *olmäq* 'to become', , which is conjugated for tense and person/number. Some examples are as follows:

I destroyed.   *xäräb eladim*

(lit: destroed did-I)

I started.	*yolä düshdüm*
	(lit: start did-I)

ADJECTIVES

Adjectives in Azeri, like in English, come before the noun. They do not agree in number with the noun they modify, so they always have the same form, as in:

good book	yäxchι kitäb
good books	yäxchι kitäb-lär

Comparative adjectives are not distinguished with a suffix and formed by adding *chox* at the start of the adjective, but the Persian compatarive suffix *tar* is used commonly, as in *gözal-tar*, and superlatives are formed by adding *läp* to the start of the adjective, as in:

the pretty house	*gözal ev*
the prettier house	*chox gözal ev*
the prettiest house	*läp gözal ev*

POSSESSION

Possession in Azeri is shown by using possessive suffix. This suffix is conjugated for person and number and follows the noun, which describes or qualifies it, as in:

my book	*kitäb-ιm*
your house	*kitäb-un*

QUESTIONS

Questions in Azeri are formed by a rise in intonation at the end of the sentence. So, unlike in English, there is no change in word order, as in:

The plane is leaving.	*haväpeymä gedir*
	(lit: plane move do-it)

The plane is leaving?   *haväpeymä gedir?*

Question words

where	*härdä*	Where is the bank? *bäng härdä-dı?*
why	*niya*	Why is the museum closed? *niya muza bäqlı-dı?*
when	*näväqt*	When does the festival begin? *näväqt jashn shuru ol-ur?*
what	*na*	What is he saying? *o na diy-ir?*
how	*najur*	How do I go there? *najür orä ged-im?*
who	*kim*	Who is she/he? *o kim-di?*
which	*hänsı*	Which is the best? *hänsı läp yäxchı-dı*

NEGATIVES

To form the negative in a sentence, the suffffix *ma* is placed after the verb root and before the personal suffix, as in:

He went to Tehran.   *o tehrän-ä get-di*

(lit: s/he to Tehran went-he)

He did not go to Tehran.   *o tehrän-ä get-ma-di*

Key Verbs

oxu-mäx   (to read)

	Present	Past	Continuous Past	Future
I	oxur-äm	oxu-dum	oxu-yur-dum	oxu-yäjäx-äm
you	oxur-sän	oxu-dun	oxu-yur-dun	oxu-yäjäx-sän
he/she/it	oxur	oxu-du	oxu-yur-du	oxu-yäjäx
we	oxur-ux	oxu-dux	oxu-yur-dux	oxu-yäjäx-dɪx
you (pl)	oxur-suz	oxu-duz	oxu-yur-duz	oxu-yäjäx-süz
they	oxur-lär	oxu-du-lär	oxu-yur-du-lä	oxu-yäjäx-lär

ye-mak (to eat)

	Present	Past	Continuous Past	Future
I	ye-yir-am	ye-dim	ye-yir-dim	ye-yajak-äm
you	ye-yir-san	ye-din	ye-yir-din	ye-yajak-sän
he/she/it	ye-yir	ye-di	ye-yir-di	ye-yajak
we	ye-yir-ik	ye-dik	ye-yir-dik	ye-yajak-ɪx
you (pl)	ye-yir-siz	ye-diz	ye-yir-diz	ye-yajak-sɪz
they	ye-yir-lar	ye-di-lar	ye-yir-di-lar	ye-yajak-lär

älmäx (to buy)

	Present	Past	Continuous Past	Future
I	älɪr-äm	äl-dɪm	äl-ɪr-dɪm	äl-äjäq-äm
you	älir-sän	äl-dɪn	äl-ɪr-dɪn	äl-äjäq-sän
he/she/it	älɪr	äl-dɪ	äl-ɪr-dɪ	äl-äjäq
we	älɪr-ɪx	äl-dɪx	äl-ɪr-dɪx	äl-äjäq-ɪx
you (pl)	älɪr-sɪz	äl-dɪz	äl-ɪr-dɪz	äl-äjäq-sɪz
they	älɪr-lär	äl-dɪ-lär	äl-ɪr-dɪ-lär	äl-äjäq-lär

gatir-mak (to bring)

	Present	Past	Continuous Past	Future
I	gatir-ir-am	gatir-dim	gatir-yir-dim	gatir-ajak-am

you	gatir-ir-san	gatir-din	gatir-ir-din	gatir-ajak-san
he/she/it	gatir-yir	gatir-di	gatir-yir-di	gatir-ajak
we	gatir-ir-ik	gatir-dik	gatir-ir-dik	gatir-ajak-ik
you (pl)	gatir-ir-siz	gatir-diz	gatir-ir-diz	gatir- ajak-siz
they	gatir-ir-lar	gatir-di-lar	gatir-ir-di-lar	gatir- ajak-lar

get-mak (to go)

	Present	Past	Continuous Past	Future
I	ged-ir-am	ged-dim	ged-ir-dim	ged-ajak-am
you	ged-ir-san	ged-dıın	ged-ir-din	ged-ajak-san
he/she/it	ged-ir	ged-di	ged-ir-di	ged-ajak
we	ged-ir-ik	ged-dik	ged-ir-dik	ged-ajak-ik
you (pl)	ged-ir-siz	ged-dıız	ged-ir-diz	ged- ajak-siz
they	ged-ir-lar	ged-di-lar	ged-ir-di-lar	ged- ajak-lar

ver-mak (to give)

	Present	Past	Continuous Past	Future
I	ver-ir-am	ver-dim	ver-ir-dim	ver-ajak-am
you	ver-ir-san	ver-din	ver-ir-din	ver-ajak-san
he/she/it	ver-ir	ver-di	ver-ir-di	ver-ajak
we	ver-ir-ik	ver-dik	ver-ir-dik	ver-ajak-ik
you (pl)	ver-ir-siz	ver-diz	ver-ir-diz	ver- ajak-siz
they	ver-ir-lar	ver-di-lar	ver-ir-di-lar	ver- ajak-lar

bil-mak (to know)

	Present	Past	Continuous Past	Future
I	bil-ir-am	bil-dim	bil-ir-dim	bil-ajak-am
you	bil-ir-san	bil-din	bil-ir-din	bil-ajak-san
he/she/it	bil-ir	bil-di	bil-ir-di	bil-ajak
we	bil-ir-ik	bil-dik	bil-ir-dik	bil-ajak-ik
you (pl)	bil-ir-siz	bil-diz	bil-ir-diz	bil- ajak-siz
they	bil-ir-lar	bil-di-lar	bil-ir-di-lar	bil- ajak-lar

elamak (to do)

	Present	Past	Continuous Past	Future
I	ela-yr-am	ela-dim	ela-yr-dim	ela-yajak-am
you	ela-yr-san	ela-din	ela-yr-din	ela-yajak-san
he/she/it	elayr	ela-di	ela-yr-di	ela-yajak
we	ela-yr-ik	ela-dik	ela-yr-dik	ela-yajak-ik
you (pl)	ela-yr-siz	ela-diz	ela-yr-diz	ela- yajak-siz
they	ela-yr-lar	ela-di-lar	ela-yr-di-lar	ela- yajak-lar

Ista-mak (to want)

	Present	Past	Continuous Past	Future
I	ista-yr-am	ista-dim	ista-yr-dim	ista-yajak-am
you	ista-yr-san	ista-din	ista-yr-din	ista-yajak-san
he/she/it	ista-yr	ista-di	ista-yr-di	ista-yajak
we	ista-yr-ik	ista-dik	ista-yr-dik	ista-yajak-ik
you (pl)	ista-yr-siz	ista-diz	ista-yr-diz	ista- yajak-siz
they	ista-yr-lar	ista-di-lar	ista-yr-di-lar	ista- yajak-lar

MEETING PEOPLE

Hello.

säläm

Goodbye.

xüdä-häfiz

Yes.

bali

No.

yox/xeyir

Excuse me.

bäqıshlıyın

Please.

lutfan

Thank you.

mamnun

Many thanks.

chox mamnun

OK.

Olsun/yäxchı

Do you mind?

eybi yox-dı?

That's OK

xähish eleyram

GREETINGS & GOODBYES

Verbal greetings in Azeri are usually accompanied by hand shaking and sometimes kissing on the cheek with the same sex. Greetings with the opposite sex are just verbal and more formal than with the same sex.

Good morning.

säbähız xeyir

Good day (noon).

günüz xeyir

Good afternoon.

äxshä-ız xeyir

Good evening.

gejüz xeyir

Hello.

säläm

Goodbye.

xüdä häfiz

Civilities

Thank you (very much).

(chox) mamnun

You're welcome.

xähish eleyram

Excuse me/Sorry. (pol)

bäqıshlıyın

May I/Do you mind?

eybi yoxdı?

How are you?

häluz najür di?

Fine!

yäxchı yäm

Not bad!

pis dovuram

You have gone to a lot of trouble.

chox zahmat chakibsiz

Let's go.

buyurun gedak

Please sit down

lutfan uturuz

Correct!

düz dı

That will do.

bas di

Do you understand?

mutavajjeh siz?

Yes, I understand.

bali düshunır am

No, I don't understand.

yox düshunmır am

Please wait a while

lutfan bir zarra sabre eliyin

FIRST ENCOUNTERS

How are you?

najürsüz?

Fine. And you?

yäxchıyäm. sız najürsüz?

What is your name?

ädız nadi?

My name is … .

ädım … di.

I'd like to introduce you to ...

istyiram sizi ... mu'arrifi eliyam

I'm pleased to meet you.

xoshbaxt am

I'm a friend of (Ali).

man alinin dostıyäm.

His/her name is ... .

ädı...di

MAKING CONVERSATION

Do you live here?

bırdä zındagi eliyirsiz?

Where are you going?

härä gedirsiz?

What are you doing?

na eliyirsiz?

What do you think (about ...)?

(....moridinda) na fikr eliyirsiz?

Can I take a photo (of you)?

(sizdan) aks tutäbilaram

What is this called?

bunun ädı nadi?

It is beautiful.

gözal di

It's very nice here.

chox yäxchı dı

We love it here.

biz bırdän xoshumuz galir

What a cute baby!

na gozal ushäq dı!

Are you waiting too?

sizda müntazirsiz?

That's strange!

ajib di!

That's funny (amusing)

gülmali di

Are you here on holiday?

bırä tatilätä galibsiz?

I'm here ... .

man ... bırdäyäm

for a holiday

tatilät-ıchın

on business

tijärat-ichin

to study

tahsil-ichin

How long are you here for?	I've been here (three days).
bırdä naqadr qäläjäxsız?	*man (üch gün) di bırdäyäm*
I'm here for .... weeks/days.	This is my first visit to (Tabriz).
man bırdä .... qäläjäxäm	*bu manim avvalin safarim Tabriza di*
Do you like it here?	Are you here on your own?
bırdän xoshuz galir?	*siz bırdä tak siz?*
We like it here very much.	I'm here with my friend
biz bırdän chox xoshumuz galir	*man bırdä dostumınän äm*
Where are you staying?	Thanks. I don't smoke.
hardä qälirsız?	*mamnun. man sigär chakmam*
How long have you been here?	I will call you later.
necha muddatdi bırdäsız?	*sora sana zang vır-räm*

USEFUL PHRASES

Sure.	It's possible.
hatman.	*mümkin di*
Just a minute.	It's not possible.
bir daqiqa sabr eliyin	*mümkin deyir*
It's OK.	Look!
eybi yoxdı	*bäx!*
It's important.	Listen/Listen to this!
möhümm di	*guläx äs/bınä guläx äs*
It's not important.	I'm ready.
möhümm dagil	*man ämädiyam*

Are you ready?

müvaffaq oläsız!

siz ämädä siz?

Just a second!

Good luck!

bir lahza sabr eliyin!

NATIONALITIES

Where are you from?

irland

siz härälı sız?

Japan

I'm from ... .

zhäpon

man ... dan am.

Spain

Australia

ispäniyä

ustäräliyä

Sweden

Austria

su,ed

otrish

the USA

Canada

ämrikä

känädä

I come from ... .

England

Man ....dan galmisham

ingilis

I live in ... .

Europe

man ... dä zindagi eliyram

urupä

the city

Germany

shahr

älmän

the countryside

India

kand/kat

hind

the mountains

Ireland

däq

the seaside

sähil/daryä qıräqı

the suburbs of ...

... in homasi

a village

bir kand/kat

CULTURAL DIFFERENCES

How do you do this in your country?

bunı kishvarüzda najur eliyirsiz

Is this a local or national custom?

bu rasm mahalidi yä milli?

I don't want to offend you.

Istamiram siza ehtirämsızlıx eliyam

I'm sorry, it's not the custom in my country.

müta'ssifam, bu manim kishvarimda rasm deyir

I'm not accustomed to this.

man bunä ädatim yoxdı

I don't mind watching, but I'd prefer not to participate

bäxmäqınn ishkälı yoxdı, vali tarjih veriram shirkat elamiyam.

In my country, we ...

manim kishvarimda, biz ...

My culture/religion does not allow me to..

manim farhang/mazhab im ijaza vermaz...

do this

bu ishi goram

drink/eat this

buni icham/yiyam

AGE

How old are you.?

sinnüz necha di?

I'm ... years old.

sinnim ... dı

How old do you think I am?.

fikr elirsiz sinnim nechadi?

I think you are ... years old.

fikr eliram sinnüz ... dı

How old is your son/daughter

oqlun/qızun sinni nechadi?

He/she is ... years old.

onun sinni nechadi?

(See Numbers & Amounts, for your age.)

OCCUPATION

Where do you work?	vakil
härdä ishlayirsiz?	mechanic
What (work) do you do?	mikänik
na ish görürsüz?	nurse
I am a/an	parastär
man ... am	office worker
artist	kärmand
hünarmand	scientist
businessperson	dänishmand
täjir	secretery
doctor	münshi
döktür	student
engineer	dänishju/shägird
mahandis	teacher
factory worker	müallim
kärgar	waiter
farmer	qärson
kashävarz/akinchi	writer
journalist	nevisanda
ruznäma chi	I'm ... .
lawyer	man ... am

unemployed	business
bikär	*tijärat*
retired	engineering
bäznishasta	*mahandisi*
I'm self-employed.	languages
manim shuqlum äzäd dı	zabän/*dil*
Do you like your job?	law
shuqluzdän xoshuz galir?	*huquq*
What are you studying?	medicine
(siz) na*oxuyursuz?*	*pezeshki*
I'm studying	Persian
man ... oxuyuräm	*färsı*
art	science
hünar	*ulum*
arts/humanities	teaching
ulume insäni	*tadris*

RELIGION

What is your religion?	Catholic
mazhabüz nadi?	*kätolik*
I am (a)	Christian
man ... am	*masihi*
Buddist	Hindo
budäyi	*hindu*

Jewish	I'm not religious.
yahudi	*man mazhabi deyiram*
Muslem	I believe in God.
müsalmän	*man ällähä mö'taqidam*

FEELINGS

I'm	*xoshhäl*
man ... am	sad
angry	*närähät*
asabäni	sleepy
happy	*yuxulu*
shad/xoshhäl	sorry (condolence)
hungry	*müta'assif*
äj	sorry (regret)
thirsty	*peshmän*
susuz	Worried
tired	*nigarän*
xasta	Are you hot?
Are you ...?	*sizichin istidi?*
(siz) ... suz?	Are you in a hurry?
happy	*sizin ajala värızdı?*

LANGUAGE DIFFICULTIES

Do you speak English?

(siz) ingilisi bäshänrsız?

Yes, I do.

bali, bäshänräm

No, I don't.

yox, bäshärmıräm

Does anyone speak English here?

bırdä biri ingilisi dänıshır?

I speak a little.

man bir zarra bashänräm

Do you understand?

uüshünürsüz?

I understand.

düshünmüram

Could you speak more slowly?

olär yäväshtar dänıshäsız?

Could you repeat that?

olär onı tikrär eliyasiz?

Please write it down.

lütfan onı yäzın

How do you say ...?

... ni najür diyarsiz?

What does ... mean?

... nın ma'nisi nadi?

What languages do you speak?

hänsı dillari bäshärirsiz?

I speak (English) and (German).

man (ingilisi) nan (älmäni) dänıshıräm

I don't speak Azeri

man äzari dänıshırmıräm

Do you have an interpreter?

(siz) mütarjim vänzdı?

Please point to it in this book.

lütfan unı bu kitäbdä nishän verin.

Finding Your Way

Where is the ...?

... härdä dı?

bus station

terminäl

train station

qätär istgähı

the city centre

shahrün markazi

the bus stop

otubus istgähı

Excuse me, can you help me please?

bäqıshläyın, olär lütfan mana kömak

eliyasiz?

I'm looking for ... .

man ...ichin äxtänräm

How do I get to ...?

najür eliyabilaram ...a gedam?

Is it far from here?

o bırdän uzäx dı?

Where are we now?

biz alän hardä yıx?

What's the best way to get there?

behtarin yol orä getmaga nadi?

Can I walk there?

eliyabilaram orä piyäda gedam

Can you show me (on the map)?

olär (naqshada) mana nishän verasan?

What time does the ... leave/arrive?

... hänsı sä'at harekat elir/yetishir?

aeroplane

haväpeymä

bus

otubus

train

qätär

What ... is this?

bu hänsi ... di?

street

xiyäbän

city

shahr

village

kand

Directions

turn ...	in front of
dönün ...	*qäbäqındä*
at the next street	far
obiri xiyäbandä	*uzäq*
at the traffic lights	near
chıräq bäshındä	*yoxun*
at the roundabout	opposite
meydändä	*muqäbil*
To the right.	here
säq tarafa	*bırä*
To the left.	there
sol tarafa	*orä*
It's two street down	north
iki xiyäbän äshäqı dı	*shumäl*
You can go on foot.	south
eliyabilarsiz piyäda gedasiz	*junub*
go straight ahead.	East
mostaqim gedin	*sharq*
behind	west
däl	*qarb*

BUYING TICKET

Where can I buy a ticket?	bilit ushäq-ıchın
man *hardä eliyabilaram bilit älam?*	1st class
We want to go to ...	*daraja yek*
biz istirik ...-a gedak	2nd class
Do I need to book?	*daraja do*
läzim di ki rezerv eliyam?	How long does this trip take?
I'd like to book a seat to ...	bu *mosäfirat naqadr tul chakar?*
(man) bir yer ...ichin istiram	I'd like a window seat, please
It is full.	*lütfan, bir sandali penjara kanärındä istir*
dolı dı	I require a ... meal.
Can I get a stand-by ticket?	*(man) bir ... qazä istiram*
eliyabilaram bir liste intizär bilit äläm	hot
I'd like ...	*isti*
(man) *... istiram*	with meat
a one-way ticket	*atinan*
bir tarafa bilit	I'd like to ... my ticket
a return ticket	*istiram bilitimi ... eliyam*
iki tarafa bilit	cancel
two tickets	*kansil*
iki dana bilit	change
a student's fare	*avaz*
bilite dänishjuyi	confirm
a child's fare	*känfirm*

AIR

Is there a flight to Esfahän tonight?	*manim vasäyilim yetis-miyib*
bu geja isfähänä parväz vänzdı?	airport tax
Is this a nonstop flight?	*avärize furudgäh*
bu parväz bidune tavaqquf dı?	arrivals
What is the flight number?	*vurud*
parväzun shumärasi necha di?	departure
Can I go to the airport by bus?	*harakat*
eliyabilaram otubusınan furudgähä gedam?	domestic
Is there a departure tax here?	*däxili*
avarize xuruj värdı?	exchange
When is the next flight to Shiraz?	*ta'viz*
galan *parväz shirazä näväxt dı?*	flight
How long does this flight take?	*parväz*
bu parväz naqadr tul chakar?	gate
What time do I have to be at the airport?	*dare xuruji*
hänsı sä'ät garak furudgähdä oläm?	international
Where should I claim my baggage?	*beynalmilali*
härdän garak vasäyilimi tahvil äläm?	passport
I'd like to check in my luggage.	*gozarnäma/päsport*
istiram vasäyilimi tahvil veram	plane
What's the charge for each excess kilo?	*haväpeymä*
har kilo *izäfa bär necha di?*	

My luggage hasn't arrived

AT CUSTOMS

This is all my luggage.

manim kulli vasäyilim budı

May I go through?

gecha billam?

I didn't know I had to declare it.

bilmirdim ki garak bunı ittilä' veram

May I call my embassy/consulate?

olär sefärat/konsulgarima telfun eliyam?

BUS & COACH

Where is the bus stop?

otubus istgähı härdädı?

Which bus goes to ...?

hänsi otubus ...-a gedir?

Do you stop at ...?

(siz) ... -da tavaqquf vänzdı?

(Two) tickets, please

lütfan, (iki dana) bilit

Can we smoke in this bus?

olär bu otubusdä sigär chakak?

Does this bus go to ...?

bu otubus ... -ä gedir?

How often do buses come?

otubuslär näväxt näväxt galirlar?

What time is the ... bus?

...otubusı näväxt galir?

next

galan/ba'di

first

avval

last

äxir

Could you let me know when we get to .

olär ... -ä yetishanda mana diyasiz?

Where do I get the bus for ...?

hardä eliyabilaram ...otubusınä minam

I want to get off.

(man) istiram piyäda oläm

TRAIN

Where is the train station?

bu ...-nin sakkusı dı?

qätär istgähı härdädı?

Do I have to change the train?

What is the next station?

(man) garak qatärı avaz eliyam?

istgähe ba'di hänsi di?

Do you mind if I smoke/put the window down?

Does this train stop at Maraghe?

bu qätärun märäqädä tavaqquf vändı?

eybi vär (man) sigär chakam/penjarani äshäqı chak

The train is cancelled.

I can't find my ticket/train/platform.

qätärın harakati kansil oldı

(man) eliyabilmiram bilit/qätär/sakkumı täpäm

The train is delayed.

qätärun ta'xir vändı

I want to get off at ...

How long will it be delayed?

(man) istiram ... dä piyäda oläm

na qadar ta'xir vändı?

platform number

How long does the trip take?

sakkunun shumärasi

musäfirat na qadar tul chakar?

ticket collector

Is that seat taken?

bazrase bilit

o birinün yeri di?

railway

Is this the platform for...?

räh ähan

TAXI

Is this taxi free?

bu ädres

bu täksi xäli di?

the airport

Please take me to ...

furudgäh

lütfan mani ... -ä äpärun

the city centre

this address

shahrün markazina

the railway station

räh ähana

How much is the fare?

kiräya na qadar di?

Do you get extra for luggage?

vasäyilichin izäfä älırsız?

Are you going to...?

(siz) ...-a gedirsiz?

Do you have change of 100 Toman?

(siz) yuz tüman xurd vänzdı?

Please don't take any other passengers

lütfan äyrı mosäfir mindirmiyin

How much do I owe you?

naqadar garak siza veram?

Continue!

idäma verin!

The next street to the left/right.

galan *xiyäbändä dönün sol/säq tarafa*

Please slow down.

lutfan yäväsh gedin

Please wait here.

lütfan bırdä müntazir olun

Stop here!

bırdä *säxlıyın*

Stop at the corner.

bu gushadä säqlıyın

CAR

Where can I rent a car?

hardä eliyabilaram bir mäshın kiräya eliyam?

How much is it daily/weekly?

haftada/äydä na qadar olär?

Does that include insurance?

bu bimiya da shämil olär?

Where's the next petrol station?

pompe benzine ba'di härdädı?

Please fill the tank.

lütfan bäkı doldurun

I'd like ... litres of petrol.

(man) ... litr benzin istiram

Please check the ...

lütfan ... ni check eliyin

oil

roqan/yäq

English	Translation	English	Translation
water	*su*	indicator	*rähnamä*
tyre pressure	*täyirun yeli*	leaded/regular	*ma'muli*
Can I park here?	*eliyabilaram bırdä pärk eliyam?*	lights	*chıräq*
How long can we park here?	na qadar *eliyabilarik bırdä pärk eliyak?*	main road	*asli jädda*
Does this road lead to ...?	*bu jädä ...-ä gedir?*	motorway (with tolls)	*otubän*
air	*yel*	puncture	*panchari*
battery	*bätri*	radiator	*rädiyätor*
brakes	*tormuz*	ring-road	*kamarbandi jädda*
clutch	*kıläj*	roadmap	yol *naqshasi*
driver's license	*gavähiye ränandagi*	seatbelt	*kamarband*
engine	*motor*	self-service	*selfservis*
garage	*mikäniki*	speed limit	*hadde aksare sür'at*

tyres

täyır

unleaded

Car Problems

We need a mechanic.

biz bir mekänik istirik

What make is it?

modeli nadi?

The car broke down at ...

mäshın ...-dä xäräb oldı

The battery is flat.

bätri xäli di

The radiator is leaking.

rädiyätor suräx dı

bedune sorb

windscreen

shishe ye jilo / qäbaq *shüshasi*

I have a flat tyre.

charxim panchar di

It's overheating.

jush gatirib

It's not working.

ishlamir

I've lost my car keys.

(man) *mäshınımun süvichin itirmisham*

I've run out of petrol.

(man)im *benzinim qutänb*

THEY MAY SAY
Taxi drivers may ask you: *darbast istirsan?*. It means
whether you want to hire the taxi just for yourself. If
you say *bali* 'yes', you should pay the difference for
other potential passengers.

ACCOMMODATION

FINDING ACCOMMODATION

I'm looking for a ...

(man) ... -ichin äxtäriräm

cheap hotel

ujuz hotel

clean hotel

tamiz hotel

nearby hotel

yoxun hotel

Where is the ... hotel?

...hotel härdä dı?

best

behtarin

cheapest

ujuztarin

What is the address?

ädresi härdä dı?

BOOKING AHEAD

I'd like to book a room, please.

lütfan istiram bir otäq rezerv eliyam

Do you have any rooms available?

xäli *otäq väruzdı?*

For (three) nights.

(üch) gejeychin

How much for ...?

... -ichin na qadar olär?

one night

bir geja

a week

bir hafta

two people

iki nafar

We will be arriving at ...

biz ...-da yetishajayik

My name is ...

manim ädım ... dı

Is there hot water all the time?

isti su hamisha vär?

I'm not sure how long I'm staying.

(man) mütma'in deyiram na qadar

qäläjäqäm

We'll be staying for (two weeks).   *biz (iki hafta) qäläjäqı*

CHECKING IN

In international hotels you won't have a problem in finding those who can speak English, but in small hotels the chance is very little.

Do you have any rooms available?	*dush*
xäli otäq väruzdı?	TV
Sorry, we're full.	*teliviziyon*
müta'assifäm yer yoxumuz dı	window
Do you have a room with two beds?	*penjara*
otäqe doxäba väruzdı?	Can I see it?
Do you have a room with a double bed?	*eliyabillam onı göram?*
otäqe dotaxta väruzdı?	Are there any others?
I'd like ...	*äyri otäq dä värdı?*
(man)...istiram	Are there any cheaper rooms?
a shared room	*ujuz otäqä dä värdı?*
otäqe müshtarak	Do you charge for the baby?
a single room	*ushäqlänchın dä kiräya älırsız?*
otäqe taki	can I pay by credit card
We want a room with a ...	*eliyabillam kärte e'tebärinan veram?*
biz bir otäq ...inan istirik	Do you require a deposit?
bathroom	*bey'äna da istirsiz?*
dastshuyi	How many Tomans?
shower	*necha tüman?*

Where is the manager?

müdir härdä dı?

Where is the bathroom?

dastshuyi härdä dı?

Is there hot water all day?

isti su günüz hamisha värdı?

How much for ...?

...na qadar olär?

one night

bir geja

a week

bir hafta

two people

do nafar

Is there a discount for children?

ushäqlär ıchın taxfif värdı?

It's fine. I'll take it.

yäxchı dı. (man) onı istiram

Requests & Complaints

I need a (another) ...

(man) bir ... (ızäfa) läzim värımdı

Can I use the kithänsın?

eliyabilaram äshpaz xänädän istifäda eliyam?

Is there a lift?

äsänsor värdı?

I've locked myself out of my room.

otäqımun qapısı qıfıllänıb

Do you change money here

(siz)bırdä arze xäriji älırsız?

Should I leave my key at reception?

garak kilidimi pazirishda goyäm?

Is there a message for me?

manichin peyqäm värdı?

Can I send my letters from here?

eliyabilaram nämalarimi burdän göndaram?

The key for room (12) please.

lütfan otäqe shumära on ikinün kilidi

Please wake me up at (six) o'clock.

lütfan mani sä'ät (ältıdä) oyädın

The room needs to be cleaned.

otäq garak tamiz olä

Please change the sheets.

lütfan maläfalari avaz eliyin

Can you give me an extra blanket, please?

lütfan olär mana bir izäfa patu verasiz?

Do you have a safe where I can leave my valuables?

bir gäv sanduq värızdı (man) vasäyilimi ordä goyäm?

Could I have a receipt for them?

olär olärıchın resid verasiz?

Is there somewhere to wash clothes?

libäs yumäqıchın bir yer värdı?

Can we use the telephone?

eliabilarik telfundän istifäda eliyak?

My room is too dark

manim otäqım chox qaranqulux dı

It's too cold/hot.

o chox sovux/isti dı

It's too noisy.

o chox sarosadälı dı

I can't open/close the window.

(man) eliyabilmiram penjarani achäm/bäqlıyäm

This ... is not clean.

bu ... tamiz deyir

blanket/sheet

patu/maläfa

pillow case

rubälishi

pillow

bälish

Please change them/it.

lütfan ulär/unnı avaz eliyin

I don't like this room.

(man) bu otäqdän xoshum galmir

The toilet does not flush.

sifun xäräd dı

CHECKING OUT

Can I pay with a travelers check?

eliyabilaram cheke musäfiratinan veram?

Could I have the bill please?

lütfan olärsurat hesäbı verasiz?

There's a mistake in the bill.

bir ishtibäh surat hesäbdä vardı

When do we have to check out?

näväxt garak otäqı taxliya eliyak?

I am leaving now.

(man) a'län istiram gedam

Can I leave my stuff with you until 2 o'clock

eliyabilaram vasäyilimi sä'ät ikiya qadar sizin yänızdä goyäm?

Please call a taxi for me.

lütfan bir täksi manichin chäqırın

Useful Words

air-con

kuler

clean

tamiz

key

kilid

face cloth

dastmäl

bottle of water

su botrisi

lamp

lämp

lock

qifil

mosquito coil

magas kosh

soap

säbın

toilet

tuvälet

toilet paper

käqaz tuvälet

towel

hola

water (cold/hot)

su (sovux/isti)

PAPERWORK

name	*mujarrad*
äd	married
address	*muta'hhil*
ädres	divorced
date of birth	*taläq älmish*
tärixe tavallüd	widow/widower
place of birth	biva/*dul*
mahalle tavallüd	identification
age	*kärte shinäsäyi*
sinn	passport number
sex	*shumäreye päsport/guzarnäma*
jins	visa
nationality	*vizä*
milliyat	driving license
religion	*gavähiye ränandagi*
din/mazhab	customs
profession/work	*gumruk*
shuql/ish	immigration
reason for travel	*muhäjirat*
iellate müsäfirat	holiday
marital status	*ta'tilät*
vaz'yate ta'hhol	business
single	*tijärat*

visiting relatives	*fämila bash vırmäx*

RENTING

I'm here for a room to rent	*olär onı göram?*
(man) kiräya otäqıchın galmisham	I'm looking for something close to…
Do you have any room to rent?	*(man) bir yerichin äxtäriräm ki…ä yoxun olä*
kiräyeychin otäq vänzdı?	city centre
Is there anything cheaper?	*shahrün markazi*
ujuztar shey da värdı?	beach
Can I see it?	*sähil*

THEY MAY SAY

I'm sorry. We're full.	*müta'assifam. yer yoxumuzdı*
How long will you stay?	*na qadar istirsiz qalasız?*
How many nights?	*necha geja?*
Do you have identification?	*kärte shenäsäyi vänzdı?*
Date of birth?	*tärixe tavallüd?*
Name?	*äd?*
Signature	*imzä*

AROUND TOWN

Looking For ...

Where is the ...?	meydäne shahr
... härdä dı?	cinema
bank	sinämä
bänk	hotel
consulate	hotel
konsulgari	market
embassy	bäzär
sifärat	museum
post office	muza
postxänä	police
public telephone	polis
telefune umumi	tourist information office
public toilet	säzmäne jahängardi
tuvälete umumi	
town square	

AT THE BANK

Can I use my credit card to withdraw money?	eliyabilaram pulimı bırdä tabdil eliyam?
eliyabilaram kärte e'ebäriyinan pul götüram?	Can I have smaller notes?
	olär kichik askinäs mana verasiz?
Can I exchange money here?	I want to change ...

(man) istiram … tabdil eliyam

cash/money

pul

a check

bir chak

a travellers check

bir chake musäfirati

What time does the bank open?

bänk näväxt ächär?

Where can I cash a travellers check?

härdä eliyabilaram bir chake musäfirati
naqd eliya

What is the exchange rate?

nerxe arz necha di?

Can I transfer money here from my bank?

eliyabilaram bänkımnän bırä pul intiqäl
veram?

How long will it take to arrive?

na qadar tul chakar yetisha?

How many Tomans per (dollar)?

necha tüman har dolanchın?

What is your commission?

Komisiyonüz naqadar di?

Has my money arrived yet?

pulum hanuz yetishmiyib?

Can I transfer money overseas?

eliyabilaram xärija pul intiqäl veram?

Where do I sign?

härdä imzä eliyim?

cash

naqd

cashier

sändıx

check

chak

coins

sikka

credit card

kärte e'ebäri

exchange rate

nerxe arz

identification

kärte shenäsäyi

signature

imzä

foreign currency

arze xäreji

money

pul

purchase	furush
xarid	tax
sale	mäliyät

AT THE POST OFFICE

I want to buy ...

(man) istiram ... älam

stamps

tambr

I want to send a ...

(man) istiram bir ... göndaram

letter

näma

parcel

basta

Please send it by ...

lütfan onı ...inän yolliyun

How much does it cost to send this to ...?

necha toman bunı (ostäräliyä)yä yollämäqıchın?

How much is the postage?

post hazinasi necha di?

air mail

poste haväyi

envelope

päkıt

express mail

poste ikspres

mail box

sanduqe post

pen

xudkär

postcode

kode posti

registered mail

poste sifärishi

surface mail

...yollämäqä bu na qadar hazina istar?

I would like an air-mail stamp to (USA).

(man) bir tambere haväyi (ämrikä)ichin istiram

How many Tomans to send this to (Australia)?

TELECOMMUNICATION

Could I please use the telephone?

olär telfunnän istifäda eliyam?

I want to call ...

(man) istiram ...-ä zang vıräm

The number is ...

shumära ... dı

How much does a three-minute call cost?

üch daqiqa telfun naqadar olär?

I want to make a long-distance call to Australia.

(man) istiram telfune rähe dur ostäräliyäyä vıräm

What is the area code for ...?

kode telfune ... necha di?

It's engaged.

mashqul dı

I've been cut off.

telfunum qat oldı

I need to get Internet access.

(man) internet lazim värımdı

answering machine

peyqäm gir

dial tone

zang

phone book

telfun daftari

phone box

bajjee telfun

phonecard

telfun kärtı

telephone

telfun

urgent

zaruri

Making a Call

Hello, is ... there?

alo, ... ordä dı?

Hello. (answering a call)

alo

May I speak to ...?

olär ... ınän dänıshäm?

Who's calling?

(siz) kimsiz?

It's ....

(man) ... am

Yes, he/she is here.

bali o bırdä dı

One moment, (please).

bir *daqiqa (lütfan)*

I'm sorry, he's not here.

müta'ssifam, o bırdä deyir

What time will she be back?

o *naväxt qayıdäjäx?*

Can I leave a message?

olär bir peyqäm goyäm?

Please tell her I called.

lütfan onä deyin man zäng vırdım

I'll call back later.

sorä zang vırräm

SIGHTSEEING

Where is the tourist office?

naväxt ächıx olär?

idäreye jahängardi härdä dı?

What time does it close?

Do you have a local map?

naväxt baqlänır?

(siz) naqsheye mahalli vänzdı?

What is that building?

What are the main attraction?

o *säxtmän nadi?*

görmäli yerlar härdädı?

What is this monument?

I'd like to see ...

bu *banä nadi?*

istiram ... ı göram

How old is it?

What time does it open?

onun na *qadar omr vändı?*

May we take photographs?	*qala*
olär biz aks säläx?	church/cathedral
I'll send you the photograph.	*kilisä*
sizichin aks yollaräm	cinema
Could you take a photograph of me?	*sinamä*
olär bir aks mannan säläsız?	concert
Can we come inside?	*konsert*
olär galak ichari?	crowded
Do you need an admission charge?	*shuluq*
vurudi älırsız?	museum
Is there a discount for…	*muza*
…ichin taxfif värdı?	park
children	*pärk*
ushäqlär	statue
students	*müjassama*
dänishjulär	
fort	

GOING OUT

Where to go

do you want to go…?	It's free of charge.
istirsiz …-a gedasiz?	majjäni di
How much does it cost to get in?	I like to go to…
vurudisi naqadar di?	(man) istyiram … -ä gedam

a cafe

qahva xänä

the cinema

sinämä

a restaurant

rasturän

the theatre

te'ätr

It's beautiful here.

bırä gözal di

I had a good time.

mana chox xosh gechdi

Invites

What are you doing this evening/this

weekend?

bu geja/äxere hafta na ish görajaksiz?

Would you like to go out somewhere?

istirsiz bir yera gedak?

Do you know a good restaurant?

yäxchı rasturän tänıyırsız?

Would you like to go for a meal?

istirsiz gedak qazä yiyak?

My shout (I'll buy).

man hesäb eliyajiyam

We're having a party.

bizim bir gonäxlıx värımızdı

Come along.

siz da galin

Responding to invites

Sure!

hatman

Yes, I'd love to come.

bali, chox istyiram galam

That's very kind of you.

chox lütfüz värızdı

Yes, let's. Where shall we go?

bali, gedak. härä gedak?

No, I'm afraid I can't.

yox, muta'sifäna eliyabilmam

ARRANGING TO MEET

At what time shall we meet?

naväxt birbirimizi görak?

Where shall we meet?

hardä birbirimizi görak?

Let's meet at eight o'clock.

sä'ät sakkizda birbirimizi görak

OK. See you then.

xob pas görüsharik

Sorry, I am late.

bäqıshlıyin gejikdim

Never mind!

eybi yoxdı

THEY MAY SAY	
Muväfiqam	I agree.
Hatman	Sure!
Kämilan düzdi	Very true!
Albatta	of course
Abadä	No way!
Muväfiq deyiram	I don't agree.
Düz deyir	That's not true.
Pas bujur	Is that so...!
Bali, ämmä...	Yes, but...

THEY MAY SAY
As the formal and polite style in Azeri is rich, there are

a lot of formal expressions in invitations and

responding to them. As a foreigner, you are not

expected to learn and use all of them.

mahabbatiz värdı	You are very kind.
chox mamnun	Thank you so much.
xähish eliyiram	Don't mention it.

FAMILY

QUESTIONS

Are you married?

(siz) müta'hhil siz?

Are you engaged?

(siz) nämzad siz?

How many children do you have?

(siz) necha ushäq värızdı?

How many brothers/sisters do you have?

necha bäjı/qärdäsh värızdı?

Do you live with your family?

(siz) xänävädüzınan zindagi elirsiz?

Is your husband here?

ariz bırdä dı?

REPLIES

I'm...

(man)...am

single

müjarrad

married .

müta'hhil

engaged

nämzad

widow/widower

biva/dul

I'm divorced.

(man) taläq älmıshäm

husband

ar

mother

änä

mother-in-law

qäynana

mum

nana

sister

bäjı

son

oqul

wife

arväd

daughter

qız

FAMILY MEMBERS

husband	first name
ar	kichik äd
mother	dad
änä	bäbä
mother-in-law	father in law
qäynana	qaynätä
mum	father
mämän	ätä
sister	girl
bäjı	qız
son	gradfather
oqul	böyük dada
wife	grandmother
arväd	böyük nana
daughter	Who looks after children?
qız	*kim ushäqlärdän muväzibat eliyir?*
baby	Do you have grandchildren?
körpa/baba	*sizin nava vänzdı?*
boy	What's your baby's name?
oqul	*babüzün ädı nadi?*
child	Is the baby a boy or a girl?
ushäq	*körpa oqlän dı yä qız?*

Does he/she let you sleep at night?

o goyur siz geja yätäsız?

She/he is very big for her/his age

o sennina göra chox bövük di

What a beautiful child!

na gözal ushäq dı!

She/he looks like you.

o siza oxshir

TALKING WITH CHILDREN

What's your name?

ädın nadi?

How old are you?

necha sinnün vär?

When is your birthday?

tavallüd günün naväxt dı?

Have you got brothers and sisters?

qärdäsh bäjı värundı?

Do you have a cat at your home?

evizda pishik vänzdı?

Do you go to school or kinder?

(san) madrasiya gedirsan yä kudakıstänä?

Is your teacher nice?

mu'llimun yäxchı dı?

Do you like school?

madrasadan xoshun galir?

Do you play sport?

varzish elirsan?

What sport do you play?

hänsı varzishi elirsan?

What do you do after school?

madrasadan sorä na ish görarsan?

Do you learn English?

(siz) ingilisi örganirsiz?

We speak a different language in my country.

manim kishvarimda biz äyri dil dänıshän

I don't understand you very well.

(man)   sanin sözlaruvi chox yäxchı düshünmiram

I come from very far away.

(man) chox üzäx yerdan galiram

Do you want to play?

istirsan oynıyäx?

What shall we play?

Na oynıyäx?

PETS

Do you like animals?	I have a …
(san) heyvänlärdan xoshun galir?	*(man) bir…värımdı*
What a cute (cat)!	bird
na gözal pishik di!	*qush*
What's s/he called?	Canary
ädı nadi?	*qanäri*
Is it male or female?	cat
o arkak di yä dishi?	*pishik*
How old is s/he?	fish
onun necha sinni vär?	*bälıx*
What breed is s/he?	kitten
o hänsi nizhäddän dı?	*pishik bälä*
Does s/he bite?	rabbit
o dishlar?	*doshän*
Do you have any pets?	parrot
sizin it/pishik värızdı?	*tuti*

INTERESTS

COMMON INTERESTS

What do you do in your spare time?	*(man) …dan xoshum galar.*
(san) äzäd väqtündä na ish gölarsan?	I don't like …
I like …	*(man) … dan xoshum galmaz*

Do you like ...?	*xarid*
(san) ...dan xoshuz galar?	travelling
film	*musäfirat*
film	watching TV
music	*televiziyonä bäxmäx*
musiqi	art
going out	*hünar*
gazmak	dancing
playing games	*oynämäx*
geym oynämäx	cooking
playing soccer	*äshpazi*
fotbäl oynämäx	photography
playing sport	*akkäsi*
varzish elamak	the theatre
reading books	*te'ätr*
kitäb oxumäx	writing
shopping	*yäzmäx*

STAYING IN TOUCH

Tomorrow is my last day here.	*qalam käqäz vänzdı?*
säbäh manim bırdä äxır günüm dı	What's your address?
let's swap address.	*ädresiz nadi?*
galin ädresimizi birbirimiza verak	Here's my address.
Do you have a pen and paper?	*bu manim ädresim di*

If you ever visit (Scotland) you must come and visit

agar bir gün eskätlanda galdiz, garak biza galasiz

If you come to (Melbourne) you've got a place to stay.

agar bir gün melbornä galdiz bir yer qälmäqıchın vänzdı

Do you have ane mail address?

(siz) imayl vänzdı?

Do you have access to a fax machine?

(siz) faksa dastrasi vänzdı?

I'll send you copies of photos.

akslardan siza yollaräm

Don't forget to write.

Yäduzdä gälsin mana yäzın

MUSIC

Do you like to listen to music?

musiqiya quläq äsmäqdän xoshun galar?

What kind of music do you like?

najur musiqidan xoshun galar?

Do you sing?

äväz oxursän?

Have you heard (Shajariyan)'s latest song

(shajariyän)un taza ähangin eshidibsan?

Where can we hear traditional music?

hardä eliabilarik musiqi ye asil eshidak?

KEY WORDS

band

guruhe musiqi

concert

konsert

concert hall

täläre musiqi

Drums

dümbak

famous

mashhur

Giutar

gitär

musician

naväzanda

orcestra	song writer
orkestr	*ähangsäz*
preformance	stage
ijrä	*sahna*
song	ticket
ähang	*bilit*
singer	voice
xänanda	*sas*

SPORT

Do you like sport?

(siz) varzishdan xoshuz galar?

I like playing sport.

(man) varzishdan xoshum galar

I prefer to watch rather than play sport.

(man)tarjih veriram ki tamäshächi oläm ta varzishk

Do you play ...?

(siz) ... chälärsız?

Would you like to play ...?

istirsiz ... chäläsız?

Useful Words

basketball	*qavväsi*
baskitbäl	hockey
boxing	*häki*
boks	keeping fit
diving	*tamrin elamak*

martial arts	tenis
varzishe razmi	gymnastics
soccer	*zhimnästik*
fotbäl	skiing
swimming	*iski*
shinä/*uzmak*	wrestling
tennis	*koshti*

Soccer

seat	*(siz) hänsı timüm tarafdän sız?*
sandali	I support (Piruzi).
ticket for the match	*(man) piruzinin tarafdän yäm*
bilit musäbiqeychin	What a team!
Do you like soccer?	*ajab tim di!*
fotbäldän xoshuz galar?	(Teractor) is better than the other team.
Which team do you support?	*(täräktur) o biri timnan yäxchı dı*

HOBBIES

Do you have any hobbies?	travelling
(siz) hich tafrih vänzdı?	*musäfirat*
I like…	cooking
(man)…nan xoshum galar	*äshpazi*
gardening	drawing
bäqbäni	*naqqäshi*

sewing	taking photographs
xayyäti	*akkäsi*

TALKING ABOUT TRAVELLING

Have you traveled much?	*yäxchı*
(siz) chox musäfirat eliyibsiz?	too expensive
How long have you been travelling?	*chox bähä*
(siz) na moddat di ki musäfiratda siz?	horrible
I've been travelling for (two months).	*vahshatnäk*
(man) (iki äy) dı ki musäfiratda yam	There are too many tourists there.
Where have you been?	*ordä chox turist vär*
(siz) härä gedibsiz	People are really friendly there.
I've been to…	*mardüm ordä väqe'an mehribän dılär*
(man) …ä getmisham	What is there to do in (Athens)?
What do you think of (London)?	*(äten) da na eliyabilarsan?*
nazarüz landanün moridinda nadi?	There is a good restaurant/hotel there.
I think it is…	*ordä yäxchı rasturän/hotel värdı*
fikr eleyram…di	I'll write down the details for you.
boring	*(man) juziyätin sizichin yäzäräm*
dänxmälı	The best time to go there is in (December
great	*yäxchi moqe' orä getmaka (desämr) dı*
jälib	Is it expensive there?
OK	*ordä bähälıx dı?*

BAD   Azeri

In   Azeri, swear and bad words are not as usual as in English. They are just used infighting and serious quarrels.

Damn

la'ati

Goddamnit

älläh la'at elasin

SOB

harämzäda

Idiot

ahmaq

imbecile

eshshak

THEY MAY SAY

muväfiqam	I agree.
mosallaman	Absolutely!
daqiqan	Exactly!
albatta	Of course!
aslan	No way!
muxälifam	I disagree.
düz deyir	That's not true.
bali, hatman	yes, sure!
bali, ämmä...	yes, but...
beharhäl	whatever!

SHOPPING

LOOKING FOR ...

Where can I buy ...?	market
hardä eliyabilaram ... älam?	*bäzär*
Where is the nearest ...?	souvenir shop
yoxuntarin ... härdä dı?	*kädo furushi*
barber	newsagency
äräyeshgar	*ruznäma furushi*
bookshop	optician
kitäbfurushi	*eynak furushi*
Chemist/pharmacy	shoe shop
däruxänä	*bäshmäxchı*
clothing store	stationers
lebäsfurushi	*laväzimotahrir*
general store	travel agency
furushgäh	*äzhänse musäfirati*
dry cleaner	
xoshk shuyi	

MAKING A PURCHASE

I'd like to buy ...	I don't like it.
istiram ... älam	*unnän xoshum galmir*
Do you have others?	Can I look at it?
äyrisi da vänzdı?	*olär onä bäxäm?*

I'm just looking.

olär rasid verasiz?

faqat bäxiräm

Does it have a guarantee?

How much is this?

bunun qäränti vändı?

bu *necha di?*

Can I have it sent overseas?

Can you write down the price?

Olär bunı manichin xärija yolliyäsız?

eliya bilarsiz qiymatin yäzäsız?

I'd like to return this.

Do you accept credit cards?

istiram bunı gaytäräm

kärte e,tebäri qabul elirsiz?

It's faulty.

I'll buy it.

xäräb dı

unı äläjäqäm

It's broken.

Please wrap it.

sınıb dı

lütfan onı bäqlıyuz

Can you give my money back.

Can I have a receipt?

olär pulumu gaytäräsız?

BARGAINING

I think it's too expensive.

ujuztar bir shey väruzdı?

fikr *eleyram o chox bähä dı*

I don't have much money.

It's too much for us.

(man) chox pul yoxum dı

o *bizichin chox dı*

I'll give you (2000) Toman.

Can you lower the price?

(man) (2000) tuman siza verajagam

Olär qiymatin birzarra äshäqı gatirasiz?

No more than (2500) Toman.

Its price is very high.

(2500) Tomannan chox yox

qiymati chox yuxän dı

Give me...

Do you have something cheaper?

mana...verin

a kilogram	*bir litr*
bir kilo	half
a liter	*yari*

ESSENTIAL GROCERIES

Where can I find...?	gäz *kapsulı*
hardä eliyabillam...täpäm?	honey
I'd like ...	*bäl*
(man) ... istiram	matches
battery	*kibrit*
bätri	meat
bread	*at*
chörak	milk
butter	*süt*
kara	pepper
cheese	*bibar*
panir	salt
chocolate	*duz*
shokolät	shampoo
eggs	*shämpo*
yumurta	soap
flour	*säbın*
un	sugar
gas cylinder	*shakar*

toilet paper	washing powder
käqaz tuvälet	*pudre lebäs shuyi*
toothpaste	yoghurt
xamir dandän	*qätix*

SOUVENIRES

baskets	pottery
sabad	*sufäl*
handicraft	jewllery
sanäye,e dasti	*javähirät*
miniature	silverware
miniyätor	*noqra/qümüsh*
rug	Fretwork
farsh	*münabbat käri*

CLOTHING

jacket	shirt
kot	*koynak*
jumper (sweater)	shoes
poliver	*bäshmäx*
pants	socks
shälvär	*joräb*
raincoat	swimsuit
bäräni	*mäyo*

T-shirt	Can I try it on?
tishert	*eliyabilaram oni imtähän eliyam?*
underwear	My size is...
libäse zir	*manin säyzım...di*
clothes	It does not fit.
libäs	*andäza deyir*
boots	It's too...
chakma	*chox...dı*
coat	big
pälto	*bövük*
dress	small
pirähane zanäna	*kichik*
jeans	short
jin	*qıssä*
pantyhouse	long
juräb shalväri	*uzun*
stockings	tight
juräbe zanäna	*där*
umberrla	loose
chatr	*gan*

MATERIALS

ceramic	cotton
sirämik	*katän*

hand made	*noqra/qümüsh*
dast säz	plastic
glass	*pelästiki*
shisha	silk
leather	*abrisham*
charm	sainless steel
metal	*istil*
damir	synthetic
brass	*masno'ı*
birinj	wool
gold	*pashmi/yün*
qızıl	wood
silver	*chubi*

COLOURS

dark ...	*qahveyi*
tira ...	green
light ...	*yäshıl*
roshan/ächıx ...	grey
black	*xäkestari*
qärä	orange
blue	*närinji*
äbi	pink
brown	*surati*

purple	white
banafsh	*äq*
red	yellow
qırmızı	*sän*

TOILETRIES

aftershave	*navär behdäshti*
äftersheyv	shampoo
comb	*shämpo*
däräx	shaving cream
condoms	*xamir rish*
kändom	soap
dental floss	*säbın*
naxe dandän	sissors
deodorant	*qaychi*
zidde araq	tampons
hair brush	*tämpon*
bores	tissues
razor	*dasmäl käqazi*
rishtaräsh	toothbrush
razor blade	*misväk*
tiq	toothpaste
sanitary napkins	*xamir dandän*

SMOKING

A packet of cigarettes, please.

lütfan bir basta sigär verin

Do you have a light?

kibrit vänzdı?

Do you mind if I smoke?

ishkäli yox-dı (man) sigär chakam?

Please don't smoke.

lütfan sigär chakmiyün?

Would you like a cigarette

sigär istirsiz?

cigarettes

sigär

cigarette papers

sigär käqäzı

filtered

filterli

lighter

fandak

matches

kibrit

pipe

pip

tobacco

tanbaki

SIZES & COMPARISONS

small

kichik

big

bövük

heavy

äqır

light

yüngül

more

chox

little (amount)

äz

too much/many

chox *chox*

many

chox

enough

käfi

also	a little bit
dä	bir zarra

THEY MAY SAY

buyurun.	*Can I help you?*
äyri shey da istirsiz?	*Will that be all?*
istirsiz onı bäqliyäm?	*Would you like it wrapped?*
müta'assifäna, faqat bu qälıb	*Sorry, this is the only one.*
na qadar/necha dana istirsiz?	*How much/how many would you like?*
mubärak di.	*Blessing (with the purchase)*

FOOD

breakfast

subhäna

lunch

nähär

supper

asräna

dinner

shäm

VEGETERIAN & SPECIAL MEALS

I'm a vegetarian.

(man) sabzixär äm

I don't eat meat.

(man) at yemam

I don't eat chicken or fish.

(man) tovuq yä bälıx yemam

I can't eat dairy products.

(man) labaniyyät yiyabilmam

Do you have any vegetarian dishes?

(siz) sbazixärlänchın maxsus qazä värızdı?

Does this dish have meat?

bu qazädä at värdı?

Can I get this without meat?

olär bunı bedune at verasiz

Does it contain eggs?

bundä yumurtä värdı?

I'm allergic to (peanuts).

(man) (yer bädäm)inä hassäsiyyat värımd

Is this organic?

bu tabi'l di?

EATING OUT

Table for (five), please.

miz (besh nafar) ichin lütfan

May we see the menu?

olär menonı görak?

I'd like lunch please.

(man) nähär istiram

Does the lunch come with salad?

nähär sälädinän dı?

What do you recommend?

(siz) na pishnahäd verirsiz?

What are they eating?	*olär na yiyellar?*
What's this dish?	*bu qazä nadi?*
Please bring me some ...	*lotfän manichin bir zarra ... gatirin*
salt	*duz*
water	*su*
pepper	*bibar*
bread	*chörak*
drink	*nushäba*
Do I get it myself or do they bring it to us?	*garak özümüz götürak yä bizichin gatirajaklar?*
Please bring ...	*lütfan ... gatirin*
an ashtray	*zirsigäri*
the bill	*surat hisäb*
a fork	*changal*
a glass of water	bir *livän su*
(with/without ice)	*(buzınän/ buzsuz)*
a knife	*pıchäq*
a plate	*bohqäb*

USEFUL WORDS

cup	*finjän*
fresh	*taza*
spicy	*tünd*
sweet	*shirin*
toothpick	*xeläle dandän*

TYPICAL DISHES

In the Delicatessen

How much is (a kilo of rice)?	*yumurtä*
(bir kilo düvi) necha di?	flour
Do you have anything cheaper?	*un*
ujuztar shey vänzdı?	honey
Give me (half a kilo) please.	*bäl*
lütfan (yänm kilo) mana verin	milk
bread	*süt*
chörak	pepper
butter	*bibar*
kara	salt
cheese	*duz*
panir	sugar
chocolate	*shakar*
shokolät	yoghurt
eggs	*qätıx*

AT THE MARKET

Meat & poultry

beef	*tovux ati*
öküz ati	lamb
chicken	*goyun ati*

goat	*jigar*
gechi ati	meat
veal	*at*
bizo ati	quail
heart	*bildirchin*
ürak	tongue
kidneys	*dil*
börak	turkey
liver	*hashtarxän*

Fish & Seafood

fish	prawns
bälιx	*meygu*
caviar	sardin
xäviyär	*särdin*
trout	tuna
qιzιlälä	*tone mähi*

VEGETABLES

beans	*hovuj*
lobiyä	cauliflower
cabbage	*gole kalam*
kalam	cellery
carrot	*karafs*

cucumber	onion
xiyär	*soqän*
eggplant	peas
bädımjän	*noxud*
green beans	potato
lobiyä sabz	*yerälmä*
lettuce	spinach
kähı	*isfanäj*
okra	tomato
bämiya	*pamädor*
mushroom	vegetables
qöbalak	*sabzijät*

Fruits & nuts

almond	cherry
bädäm	*giläs*
apple	conconut
älmä	*närgil*
apricot	fig
arik	*anjir*
banana	grape
moz	*üzüm*
berry	grapefruit
tut	*gripfurut*

hazelnut	pear
fındıq	*ärmud*
kiwifruit	peanut
kivi	*bädäm zamini*
lemon	pineapple
limu	*änänäs*
mandarin	pistachio
näringi	*püsta*
melon	plum
govun	*älı*
nut	pomegrante
äjil	*när*
orange	strawberry
portäxäl	*tut firangi*
peach	watermelon
hülı	*qärpüz*

Spices & Condiments

cinemon	lemon
därchin	*limu*
fruit jam	oil
muräbbä	*yäq*
garlic	olive oil
sänmsäx	*zeytun yäqı*

onions	*namak*
soqän	suger
red peppers	*shakar*
qɪrmɪzi bibar	turmeric
saffron	*särikök*
za'farän	vinegar
salt	*sirka*

DRINKS

boiled water	*shir suvɪ*
äbe jush	(cup of) tea
fruit juice	*chäy*
äb miva	with/without milk
coffee	*sütinan yä sütsüz*
qahva	with/without sugar
mineral water	*shakarinan yä shakarsiz*
äb ma'dani	water
soft drink	*su*
nushäba	yoghurt drink
tap water	*äyrän*

HIKING

Are there any tourist attractions near here?

bu *yoxunnuxdä turisti yerlar värdı?*

Where is the nearest village?

yoxuntarin kand härdädı?

Is it safe to climb this mountain?

bu däqa chıxmäx amn di?

Is there a hut up there?

yuxändä panähgäh värdı?

Do we need a guide?

biz *rähnamä läzim värımızdı?*

How long is the trail?

bu *masir naqadr tul chakar?*

Is the track well marked?

bu *masir yäxchı alämat goyulub?*

How high is the climb?

ertefäsı naqadar di?

Which is the shortest route?

qıssätarin yol hänsi dı?

Which is the easiest route?

äsäntarin yol hänsi dı?

Is the path open?

masir ächıx dı?

When does it get dark?

naväxt qaranquluxläshäjäx?

Is it very scenic?

manzarasi chox yäxchı dı?

Where can we buy supplies?

hardä eliabilarik vasäyil äläx?

On the Path

Where have you come from?

(siz) hardän galibsiz?

Does this path go to ...?

bu *yol ...-ä gedir?*

I'm lost.

(man) itmish am

altitude

irtifä'

backpack

kula poshti

binoculars

dürbün

candles

sham

to climb	naqsha
yuxän chıxmäx	mountain climbing
compass	kuhnavardi/däqä chıxmäx
qotb numä	pick
downhill	bältä
äshäqi	provisions
first-aid kit	tadärokät
ja'be komakhäye avvaliyya	rock climbing
gloves	saxranavardi
aljak	rope
guide	ip
rähnamä	uphill
hunting	yuxäri
shikär	to walk
map	yol getmak

AT THE BEACH

Can we swim here?	bälıx tutmäx
eliyabilarik bırdä üzak?	rock
Is it safe to swim here?	saxra
bırdä üzmak amn di?	sand
beach	qum
sähil	sea
fishing	daryä

snorkelling	*shenä/ozmak*
qavväsi	towel
sunblock	*hola*
kereme zidde äftäb	waterskiing
sunglasses	*eski ruye äb*
eynake äftäbi	waves
swimming	*amväj*

WEATHER

What's the weather like?	*äqır yäqısh yäqır*
havä najür di?	It's raining lightly.
Today it is ...	*äz yäqısh yäqır*
bugün hävä ... dı	It's flooding.
cloudy	*sel galir*
bulut/*abri*	autumn
cold	*päyiz*
sovux	to freeze
hot	*buz bäqlämäx*
daq	ice
warm	*buz*
isti	snow
windy	*qär*
yel	snowy
It's raining heavily.	*qärrix*

spring	typhoon
yäz	*tufän*
storm	weather
tufän	*hävä*
summer	wind
yäy	*yel*
sun	winter
gün	*qısh*

GEOGRAPHICAL TERMS

beach	forest
sähil	*jangal*
bridge	hill
körpü	*tapa*
cave	hot spring
kövül	*isti su*
cliff	house
saxra	*ev*
earthquake	island
zilzila	*jazira*
farm	lake
zami/*mazri'a*	göl/*daryächa*
footpath	mountain
ayäx *raddi*	*däq*

peak	qala
qülla	historical
river	tärixi
chay	mosque
sea	masjid
daryä	museum
valley	muza
dara	old
waterfall	qadimi
äbshär	ruin
ancient	xäräba
bästäni	shrine
church	maqbara
kilisä	statue
fortress	müjassama

FAUNA

Farm animals

calf	chicken
bizo	tovux
camel	roaster
dava	xoruz
cat	cow
pishik	öküz/inak

dog	*qäz*
it	hen
donkey	*tovux*
eshshak	horse
duck	*ät*
ördak	sheep
goat	*qoyun*
gechi	lamb
goose	*quzu*

Wild life

ant	*milchak*
qärishqä	fox
bear	*rubäh*
äyı	tülki
cockroach	lion
susk	*shir*
crocodile	monkey
kartankala/*susmär*	*meymun*
deer	mosquito
jeyrän/*ähu*	*pasha*
fish	pig
bälıx	*dovuz*
fly	rabbit

doshan	tiger
snake	babr
ilän	wolf
spider	gurt
ankabut	

Birds

bird	owl
qush/parande	bäyqush
butterfly	stork
parväna	laklak
eagle	vulture
uqäb	karkas
quail	woodpecker
bildirchin	äqäsh dalan/därkub

FIORA & AGRICULTURE

agriculture	zürgat
akin/kashävarzi	cotton
banana	pämbux
moz	crops
barley	mahsul
ärpä	farmer
corn	akinchi/ kashävarz

flower	sunflower
gül	*güna bäxän*
grapes	sultana
üzüm	*kishmish*
harvest (verb)	tobacco
bardäsht/bichmak	*tanbaki*
irrigation	tree
äbyäri/suvärmäx	*äqäj*
leaf	village
yärpäx	*kand*
planting/sowing	villager
akmak	*katdi*
rice field	wheat
düvü zamisi	*buqdä*

HEALTH

AT THE DOCTOR

Where is the ...?

  ... härdä-dı?

How do you feel?

hälun najur di?

doctor

döktür

hospital

bimärestän

chemist

däruxänä

dentist

dish dökuri/*dandänpezeshk*

I'm sick.

näxosh/*mariz am*

My friend is sick.

dostum näxosh/*mariz dı*

I need a doctor who speaks English.

(man) bir döktür läzim vänımdı ki ingilisi bäshärä

It hurts there.

orä äqriyir

I feel nauseous.

üragim bılänır

I've been vomiting.

istifräq eleyram

I feel better/worse.

hälim behtar/badtar di

Can the doctor come here?

döktür bırä galabilar?

I have caught a cold

mana sovux dayib

You May Hear

What's the matter?

na olub?

Do you feel any pain?

äqrı värin dı?

Where does it hurt?

härä äqrır?

Are you menstruating?

periyod sän?

Do you have a temperature?	*sigär chakirsan?*
tab värundı?	Do you drink?
How long have you been like this?	*mashrub icharsan?*
necha vaqt di bujur san?	Do you take drugs?
Have you had this before?	*mavadde moxadder masraf elarsan?*
qablan bujur olıbsän?	Are you allergic to anything?
Are you on medication?	*bir sheya hassasiyyat väun dı?*
däru masraf elirsan?	Are you pregnant?
Do you smoke?	*hämila san?*

AILMENTS

I'm ill.	*(man) … värımdı*
(man) näxosh/mariz am	an allergy
I can't sleep.	*hassäsiyyat*
yätäbilmiram	anaemia
I feel ...	*kam xuni*
(man) ....ehsäs eleyram	cancer
dizzy	*saratän*
gijalmak	a cold
shivery	*sovux dayma*
titramak	constipation
weak	*yubusat*
za'if	cystitis
I have ...	*kist*

a cough	lice
öskürmak	*bira*
diarrhoea	a migraine
ishäl	*migrin*
a fever	a pain
tab	*äqn*
a headache	a sore throat
bash äqn	*boqäz äqn*
a heart condition	a stomachaahe
närähati qalbi	*ma'da äqnsı*
indigestion	a toothache
su' e häzima	*dish äqnsı*
an infection	worms
ufunat	*qurd*

Useful Phrases

This is my usual medicine.	I don't want a blood transfusion.
bu *manim ma'muli därum dı*	*(man) tazriqe xon istamiram*
I have been vaccinated.	Can I have a receipt for my insurance?
(man) väksan vırmısham	*olär bimaychin mana rasid verasiz?*

WOMEN'S HEALTH

Could I be examined by a female doctor

olär xänım döktür mani mäynä eliya?

I'm pregnant.

(man) hämila yam

I think I'm pregnant.

fikr *eleyram hämila yam*

I'm on the pill.

(man) qurs yiyeyram

I haven't had my period for ... weeks.

... hafta di ki periyod olmämıshäm

I'd like to get birth control pill.

istiram ki qorse zidde hämilagi äläm

abortion

ushäq sälmäx/*siqte janin*

miscarriage

seqt

SPECIAL HEALTH NEEDS

I have ...

(man) ... vänmdı

diabet

diyäbet

asma

äsm

anaemia

kam xuni

I'm allergic to ...

(man) ...-ä hassäsiyyat vänmdı

antibiotics

äntibiyutik

aspirin

äsperin

bees

än

codeine

kode'in

dairy products

labaniyyät

penicillin

penisilin

pollen

garda

I have a skin allergy.

(man) hassasyyate pusti vänmdı

I've had my vaccinations.	*dishlamak*
(man) väksanlarimi vırmıshäm	blood test
I have my own syringe.	*äzemäyeshe xun*
(man) özümün surang värımdı	contraceptive
I'm on medication for ...	*zidde hämilagi*
(man) ... ıchın däru masraf eliram	injection
I need a new pair of glasses.	*tazriq*
(man) täza eynak lazim värımdı	injury
addiction	*yärä*
e'tiyäd	vitamins
bite (insect)	*vitämin*
sächmäx	wound
bite (dog)	*yärä*

PARTS OF THE BODY

appendix	*qän*
äpändis	bone
arm	*sümük*
qol	chest
back	*sina*
däl	ears
bladder	*guläx*
masäna	eye
blood	*göz*

finger	*riya*
bärmäx	mouth
foot	*äqız*
ayäx	muscle
hand	*azola*
al	ribs
head	*qäbırqä*
bäsh	shoulder
heart	*chiyin*
qalb	skin
kidney	*dari*
koliya	stomach
knee	*ma'da*
diz	teeth
legs	*dish*
ayäx	throat
liver	*boqäz*
jigar	vein
lungs	*rag*

AT THE CHEMIST

I need something for ...	*(man) ... ichin nüsxa läzim värımdı?*
(man) bir shey ...ichin istiram	How many times a day?
Do I need a prescription for ...?	*necha dafa har gün?*

Four times a day.	gauze
dört dafa har gün	*gäz*
Once every six hours	laxatives
har älti sä'ät bir dafa	*mülayyin*
Are there side effects?	painkillers
aväriz vändi?	*müsakkin*
antiseptic	rubbing alcohol
zidde ufuni	*alkol*
bandage	sleeping pills
bändäzh	*yuxu habbi*

AT THE DENTIST

I have a toothache.	*lasam äqrir*
(man) dishin äqrir	I don't want it extracted.
I have a hole.	*istameyram oni chakam*
dishim suräx di	Please give me an anaesthetic.
I've broken my tooth.	*lütfan mana bir bihess konande verin*
dishin sinib	Ouch!
My gums hurt.	*äx*

USEFUL WORDS

bleeding	xunrizi
blood pressure	fishäre xun
high/low	yuxärı/äshäqı
injection	tazriq
operation	amal
pill	qurs/hab
to vomit	istifräq
X-ray	aksbardäri

Useful Words

casual	job
movaqqati	*shuql/ish*
employee	occupation/trade
müstaxdim	*hirfa/ish*
employer	part-time
kärfarmä	*nima vaqt*
full-time	work experience
tamäm vaqt	*tajrübeye kär*

ON BUSSINESS

We're attending a ...	meeting
biz *... dä sherkat eliyeyrik*	*jalase*
conference	trade fair
konferäns	*namäyeshgähe bäzargäni*

I have an appointment with ...

(man) ... ınän qarär värımdı

Here's my business card.

bu manim *kärte bäzargäni dı*

I need an interpreter.

(man) bir mütarjim läzım värımdı

I need to use a computer.

(man) bir kämpiyuter läzim värımdı

I need to send a fax/an email.

(man) istiram bir faks/imeyl göndaram

Useful Words

cellular/mobile phone	exhibition
telfone hamräh/mobäyl	*namäyeshgäh*
client	manager
arbäb ruju'	*müdir*
colleague	profit
hamkär	*manfaát/sud*

ON TOUR

We're part of a group.	*tim*
biz jozve bir guruh ıx	crew
We're tourists.	*xadama*
biz turist ik	Please speak with our manager.
I'm with the ...	*lütfan müdürümüzunan dänıshun*
(man) ... nan am	We've lost our equipment.
group	biz *vasäyilimizi itirmishik*
guruh	flight
team	*parväz*

train	bus
qätär	*otubus*

PILGRIMAGE & RELIGION

What is your religion?	*(man) ällähä mö'taqidam*
süzün dinüz nadi?	Can I pray here?
I'm ...	*bırdä ibädat eliyabilaram?*
(man) ... am	Where can I pray/worship?
Buddhist	*hardä ibädat eliyabilaram*
budäyi	church
Christian	*kilisä*
masihi	funeral
Hindu	*tadfin*
hendu	God
Jewish	*älläh*
yahudi	prayer
Muslim	*du'ä/ibädat*
müsalmän	priest
I'm not religious.	*keshish*
(man) mazhabi deyiram	shrine
I believe in God.	*maqbara*

TIME, DATES & FESTIVALS

TELLING THE TIME

What time is it?

sä'ät necha di?

(It's) one o'clock.

sä'ät bir di

(It's) ten o'clock.

sä'ät on dı

Half past one.

bir *yarım dı*

Half past three.

üch *yarım dı*

It's 2.15.

sä'ät iki on besh daqiqa di

It's 20 to 12.

sä'ät yirmi daqiqa on ikiya

The bus leaves at 5.10

otubus beshi on daqiqa gechanda harekat elir

The train should arrive at 18 minutes to six

qätär garak ältıyä on sakkiz daqiqa qäländä yetisha

DAYS OF THE WEEK

The week starts at Saturday and ends inFriday. The weekend holiday is Friday.

Monday

doshanba

Tuesesday

seshanba

Wednesday

chähärshanba

Thursday

panjshanba

Friday

jüma

Saturday

shanba

Sunday

yekshanba

MONTHS

January	July
zhänviya	*zhu'iyya*
February	August
fevriya	*ut*
March	September
märs	*septämr*
April	October
ävril	*oktobr*
May	November
meh	*novämr*
June	December
zhu'an	*desämr*

The months are different from English. New year starts at 21 of March, which is the first day of *farvardin* the first month of the year.

months	starts at:
farvardin	21 March-
ordibehesht	21 April
xordäd	22 May
tir	22 June
mordäd	23 July
shahrivar	23August
mehr	23 September

äbän	23 October
äzar	22 November
dey	22 December
bahman	21 January
esfand	20 February

SEASONS

summer	winter
yäy	*qısh*
autumn	spring
päyıyz	*yäz*

DATES

People can not tell you the Christian date without looking to the calendar. All the official dates are in Persian calendar, which is solar and 364 days.

What date it is today?	this week
bugün hänsı gün di?	bu *hafta*
It's 12 Aban.	this year
äbänun on ikisi di	*bu il*
today	now
bugün	*alän*
this morning	early/late
bugün süb	*tez/gej*
tonight	this month
bu geja	bu *äy*

every hour/day/month	It takes…minutes.
har sä'ät/gün/äy	*…daqiqa chakar*
yesterday	When will you come back.
dünan	*naväxt gayıdäjäxsız?*
day before yesterday	When will it be ready?
irali gün	*o näväxt ämäda olär?*
yesterday morning	I'll stay for four days/weeks.
dünan süb	*(man) dord hafta qälajäqäm*
last night	tomorrow
dünan geja	*säbäh*
last week	day after tomorrow
gechan *hafta*	*bir gün*
last month	tomorrow morning
gechan äy	*säbäh süb*
last year	tomorrow afternoon
gechan il	*säbäh asr*
in 20 minutes	tomorrow evening
yirmi daqiqada	*säbäh geja*
three hours from now	next week/month
üch *sä'ät sorä*	galan *hafta/äy*
How many hours does it take?	next year
necha sä'ät chakar?	*galan il*
It takes…hours.	soon/right away
…sä'ät chakar	*tezliginan/foran*

afternoon	noon
asr	*zöhr*
dawn	sunrise
sahar	*tulu'*
day	sunset
gün	*qurub*
early	second (time)
tez	*säniya*
midnight	sometimes
geja yänsı	*ba'zi växt*
morning	fast/slow
süb	*tünd/künd*
night	
geja	

NUMBERS & AMOUNTS

CARDINAL NUMBERS

1	*bir*
2	*iki*
3	*üch*
4	*dörd*
5	*besh*
6	*ältı*
7	*yeddi*
8	*sakkiz*
9	*doqquz*
10	*on*
11	*on bir*
12	*on iki*
13	*on üch*
14	*on dord*
15	*on besh*
16	*on ältı*
17	*on yeddi*
18	*on sakkiz*
19	*on doqquz*
20	*yirmi*
21	*yirmi bir*
22	*yirmi iki*

30	otuz
40	qırx
50	alli
60	ätmısh
70	yetmish
80	hashtäd
90	doxsän
100	yuz
200	iki yuz
300	üch yuz
400	dörd yuz
500	besh yuz
600	älti yuz
700	yeddi yuz
800	sakkiz yuz
900	doqquz yuz
1000	min
2000	iki min
2200	üch min
45	dörd min
167	yüz ätmısh yeddi
1320	min üch yüz yirmi
1999	min doqquz yuz doqsän yeddi
14800	on dord min sakkiz yüz

ORDINAL NUMBERS

1st	avval
2nd	ikimji
3rd	üchümji
6th	ältımjı
13th	on üchümjı
20th	yirminji
1/2	yari
all	hämmısı
none	hech

EMERGENCIES

Help!	Watch out!
kömak!	*muväzib ol!*
Stop!	It's an emergency.
ist!	*iztiräri di*
Go away!	Could you help us please?
Radd ol!	*olär lütfan biza kömak eliyasiz?*
Thief!	Could I please use the telephone?
oqrı!	*olär lütfan telfunnän istifäda eliyam?*
Fire!	Where is the toilet?
ot!	*tuvälet härdä dı*

POLICE

Call the police!

polisi chäqırın!

Where is the police station?

edäreye polis härdä dı?

We want to report an offence.

biz *istirik bir jurmi guzärish verak*

I've been robbed.

vasäyilimi oqurlıyıblär

My ... was/were stolen.

... im oqurlänıb

backpack

kula poshti

bags

kif

handbag

kif dasti

money

pul

papers

madärık

travellers check

chake musäfirati

passport

päsport

wallet

kife pul

My possessions are insured.

vasäyilim bima di

I'm sorry/I apologise.

ma'zarat istiram

I didn't realise I was doing anything wrong.

(man) bilmadin ki bu ish ishtibäh dı

I didn't do it.

(man) bu ishi görmamisham

We are innocent.

biz bigünäh ıx

We are foreigners.

biz *xärijiyik*

I wish to contact my embassy/consulate

(man) istiram sefärat/konsulgariminan tämäs tutäm

Can I call someone?

eliyabilaram birina zang vıräm?

Can I have a lawyer who speaks English?

eliyabilaram bir vakila tutäm ki ingilisi dänıshır?

I understand.

düshüniram	prison
I don't understand.	*zindän*
düshünmiram	trial
arrested	*dädgäh*
dastgir	What am I accused of?
cell	*(man) nayichin müttaham am?*
sellul	anti-government activity
embassy/consulate	*fa'äliyyate zidde dolat*
sefärat/konsulgari	assault
fine (payment)	*aziyyat*
jarima	illegal entry
guilty	*vurude qeyre qänuni*
muqassir	murder
lawyer	*qatl*
vakil	rape
not guilty	*tajävüz*
bigünäh	robbery/theft
police officer	*oqurrux*
ma'mure polis	working with no permit
police station	*ish bedune ijäza*
idäre ye polis	

About the author

I am a self published author, language manager, linguist and lecturer in Iranian languages including Persian (Farsi & Dari), Pashto, and Turkic languages including Azeri and Turkish. I completed my Ph D in Linguistics in Melbourne, Australia. My dissertation was the study of comparative grammars of Persian, Azeri, Turkish and English. I have been a lecturer in Persian Linguistics, Persian as a second language and English as a second language for several years in universities. I have published severa books, phrasebooks, grammar books, dictionaries and culture books. I am a native speaker of Azeri and Persian and speak Turkish, Dari and Pashto as well.

For my other books, click here:

Yavar Dehghani.Books.Amazon.com

My website (www.yadehghani.com):

yadehghani.html

111